THE NUTCRACKER BALLET BOOK

By
K. A. Devlin

Dedicated to my favorite Sugar Plum Fairy,
Julia,
who fell in love with ballet at the age of two, and worked hard every year
thereafter rehearsing and studying dance. She would not even let a
worldwide pandemic stop her from reaching her goal, even if it meant
dancing in her dream role while wearing a face mask. Her grace and
determination serve as an inspiration to me and countless others.

Author's "Director's Notes"
Welcome to this "production" of The Nutcracker Ballet!

This classical ballet started as a short fairy tale written by German author, E.T.A. Hoffman in 1816. A famous French ballet master had the idea to make the story into a ballet, and the music was composed by Pyotr Tchaikovsky. The ballet was first performed in Russia in 1892. Although it was not very popular then, it has now become a beloved traditional Christmas ballet, being performed every year all over the world by famous ballet companies as well as by local dance schools.

When performed as a ballet, this story is told without words--just music and dance. Each production of the Nutcracker Ballet is somewhat different. While the music and plot remain the same, the characters and sets often differ slightly. For example, one production may have a Rat Queen instead of a Mouse King, while a different company's production may portray Fritz as a sister instead of a brother. The Merlitons may be called Marzipans, or the Sugar Plum Fairy may dance alone or with a Cavalier instead of the Nutcracker Prince. Productions can differ from one to another in many ways, depending on the imagination, resources, and available dancers for each performing group.

This author took her daughter, Julia, to see her first Nutcracker Ballet at the age of two! Julia loved it so much that she declared that she would one day be the Sugar Plum Fairy. She began dance lessons the next year. By age 7, she began performing in her dance school's production of The Nutcracker each year, dancing in most of the roles captured in this book. As a senior in high school, she finally achieved her goal as she was cast in the role of the Sugar Plum Fairy! It is with that beautiful dream performance in mind that this book was created. May it spark the same joy and wonder in the readers as Julia had that first time she saw this wonderful ballet.

It's Christmas Eve!
Clara's family is getting ready
for their Christmas party.

Mother and Father check to see that everything is ready, while Clara's little brother, Fritz, tries to scare her with a fake mouse.

Soon, the party guests arrive.

Everyone has fun playing games
and dancing.

Mysterious Uncle Drosselmeyer arrives,
bringing gifts and some magical dancing dolls.

Everyone is amazed to see the life-sized dolls dance!

Uncle Drosselmeyer then gives gifts
to all the children.

He presents Clara with
a very special gift--
a nutcracker!

The children all play and
dance with their new toys,

but Fritz is jealous and tries to grab the special gift away from Clara, breaking off the nutcracker's head!

Uncle Drosselmeyer uses a scarf and
a little magic to fix the nutcracker.

Clara is happy again!

The party is over now and all the guests leave.

Clara places her nutcracker by the
Christmas tree and falls asleep on the sofa.

When the clock strikes midnight,
the mice come out to play.

Clara wakes up and is surrounded by mice!

Suddenly, the Nutcracker magically becomes a life-sized soldier! He marches in with an army of toy soldiers to rescue Clara from the mice.

The evil Mouse King arrives and leads the mice in an epic battle against the Nutcracker!

While they are fighting, Clara has a great idea!
She throws her slipper at the Mouse King.
When he turns around to see who threw the slipper,
the Nutcracker strikes him from behind and defeats
the Mouse King--

but the Nutcracker has been hurt too and falls down.
Clara feels so upset that she faints.

When she awakens, Clara is surprised to find that
the Nutcracker has magically become a real-life prince!
He takes her on a journey
through the enchanted forest.

They are met by the Snow Queen and her dancing snowflakes, who guide them to the Kingdom of Sweets!

In the Kingdom of Sweets,
they are welcomed by the Sugar Plum Fairy.
Clara tells her the story of how she helped to defeat
the evil Mouse King by throwing her slipper.

The Sugar Plum Fairy rewards Clara for her bravery
with a tiara, making her a princess!
Friends from all over the world gather to celebrate
and perform a special dance in Clara's honor.

The Spanish Princess arrives
with a gift--chocolates from Spain!
She performs a beautiful dance,
snapping her fan and clacking her castanets.

The Arabian Princess also
brings a gift--Arabian coffee!
She performs an enchanting dance with
amazing balance, stretches, and bends.

The Russian Prince brings
Clara some peppermint candy.
He performs a thrilling dance with
many big exciting leaps and spins!

The Chinese Prince and Princess bring Clara tea from China! They perform a lively dance filled with high jumps and low bows.

The French Merlitons dance "en pointe" (on their toes) with pipe flutes and bring fancy french pastries for Clara and the Prince.

Mother Ginger enters and
surprises everyone when
her little bonbon children
come out from under her big skirt!

The Dew Drop Fairy arrives
next, bringing flowers and dancing
a fancy waltz with her friends.

The Sugar Plum Fairy
performs the most special dance
of all, with lots of whirls and twirls!

The Nutcracker Prince joins her and they perform a beautiful dance together with lifts and spins.

They then invite Clara to dance,
and all the other dancers join in,
but strangely, Clara starts to
yawn and falls asleep.

Clara awakens, realizing that it is Christmas morning, and everything that happened was just a dream. She smiles, remembering her wonderful dream, and gives her Nutcracker a big hug!

THE
END

Bonbon

Soldier

Mouse

Arabian Merchant

Spanish Chocolate

Doll

Sugar Plum Fairy

Russian Peppermint

Arabian Princess

Chinese Princess

Snowflake

Spanish Princess

Flower

Made in United States
Troutdale, OR
11/08/2024

24535318R00026